# Art Nouveau
## floral designs

· THE TREASURY OF DECORATIVE ART ·

# Art Nouveau
## floral designs

EUGENE GRASSET

INTRODUCTION BY
# LAURA SUFFIELD

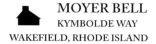

**MOYER BELL**
KYMBOLDE WAY
WAKEFIELD, RHODE ISLAND

*Frontispiece*
**COLUMBINE**


*Page 6*
**DANDELION**

Published by Moyer Bell

Text and layout copyright © 1997 Studio

First Edition
LIBRARY OF CONGRESS
CATALOGING-IN-PUBLICATION DATA

Grasset, Eugène, 1841-1917
    Art nouveau floral designs / Eugène Grasset.
        p.    cm.    — (The treasury of decorative art)
    "Contains a selection of plates from La plante et ses applications
ornamentales, by Eugène Grasset published by E. Lyon-Claesen
Bruxelles, 1897.
    ISBN 1-55921-160-1 (alk. paper)
    1.  Decoration and ornament—Plant forms.   2.  Decoration and
ornament—Art nouveau.   I.  Grasset, Eugène, 1841-1917.  Plante et
ses applications ornamentales.  II. Title.  III. Series.
NK 1560.G69  1997
745.4—dc21                                                            97-6212
                                                                        CIP


Designed by xheight design limited


Printed and bound by Oriental Press, (Dubai)


Distributed in North America
by Publishers Group West, P.O. Box 8843, Emeryville.

# CONTENTS

INTRODUCTION                    7

PLATE 1                        12
**Arrow-head**

PLATE 2                        14
**Bryony**

PLATE 3                        16
**Chestnut Tree**

PLATE 4                        18
**Cyclamen**

PLATE 5                        20
**Geranium**

PLATE 6                        22
**Gourd**

PLATE 7                        24
**Gourd**

PLATE 8                        26
**Iris**

PLATE 9                        28
**Five-leaved Ivy**

PLATE 10                       30
**Jonquil**

PLATE 11                       32
**Lilac**

PLATE 12                       34
**Lily of the Valley**

PLATE 13                       36
**Monkshood**

PLATE 14                       38
**Nasturtium**

PLATE 15                       40
**Nasturtium**

PLATE 16                       42
**Oak**

PLATE 17                       44
**Periwinkle**

PLATE 18                       46
**Poppy**

PLATE 19                       48
**Poppy**

PLATE 20                       50
**Umbellated Rush**

PLATE 21                       52
**Snowdrop**

PLATE 22                       54
**Snowdrop**

PLATE 23                       56
**Sorb**

PLATE 24                       58
**Sorb**

PLATE 25                       60
**Sunflower**

PLATE 26                       62
**Waterlily**

# INTRODUCTION

*La Plante et ses Applications Ornementales*, the original publication from which this selection of plates is drawn, marks one of the finest achievements of the Swiss painter, sculptor, designer and illustrator Eugène Grasset (1845-1917), a major pioneer in the field of Art Nouveau design and illustration. Recognized in its own time, it is still today acknowledged as a major source of Art Nouveau patterns and motifs.

The range and versatility of Grasset's talent was outstanding. As a child his interest in art was encouraged by his father, a sculptor and wood inlayer. At an early age Grasset was captivated by Gustav Doré's famous book illustrations to *Orlando Furioso*, *Don Quixote* and Dante's *Inferno*. After training as an architect in Zurich and Lausanne, he concentrated upon developing skills as a topographical watercolourist during a formative trip to Egypt in 1866-67. On his return to Switzerland he began designing sculpture for the façade and interior of the theatre at Lausanne. It was here that he was probably introduced to the celebrated French architect, engineer and archaeologist, Viollet-le-Duc, whose theories of architectural ornament and designs for decorative ironwork were a major influence on Grasset's own early studies in these fields. In 1871 Grasset moved to Paris where his career may be seen as truly beginning. The range of designs he produced – for furniture, textiles, typography, stained glass and wallpaper – demonstrated a breadth and creativity which was to last throughout his long and distinguished career (in 1901 he was made a Chevalier of the Légion d'Honneur). Grasset not only worked as a teacher of design at the Ecole Normale d'Enseignement du Dessin, Paris, but was also a prominent poster artist whose work bears comparison with that of Chéret and Mucha. Posters such as the *Librairie Romantique*, produced in 1887 for the publisher E. Monnier, achieved instant popularity and are still reproduced today. As a poster-maker Grasset's influence was particularly strong in America due to the work of his pupil Louis John Rhead and his own celebrated covers for *Harper's* magazine.

Accounts of Grasset's early life written by friends and colleagues such as Octave Uzanne, the founder of the influential journal *L'Art et l'Idée*, stress his interest in the art of Japan and the Middle Ages as well as his enduring fascination with the work of Viollet-le-Duc. These sources are now recognized as vital factors in the development of the style which was later to be known as *l'Art Nouveau*, so called after the famous Parisian shop of that name opened by Samuel Bing in 1895. In the 1870s, however, Grasset was a pioneer in the application of Japanese and medieval motifs to illustration and design. His closest counterpart is probably the celebrated English illustrator Walter Crane who from as early as 1865 acknowledged the influence of Japanese art in his work, and whose emphasis on the primacy of line and the stylization of natural forms is comparable to Grasset's. These two artists were responsible for some of the finest book illustrations to be produced in the 1870s and 1880s.

Grasset was fortunate in making the acquaintance of Charles Gillot, son of the well-known printer Firmin Gillot (inventor of the *gillotage* printing process). The young Gillot proved an enlightened supporter of the artist, commissioning designs and furniture for his house and studio. In 1881 he proposed that Grasset should illustrate the legendary story of Charlemagne, the *Histoire des Quatre fils d'Aymon* published in 1883, which must be seen as one of the artist's finest works. According to Grasset's friend Uzanne it was 'one of the most beautiful books of the century'. The splendour of these illustrations lies in the perfect integration of the central scenes within elaborate and detailed borders which combine medieval and Celtic interlacing with a Japanese approach to spatial arrangement. Many of the illustrations contain floral elements, all derived from recognizable species but stylized to become part of the decorative structure. In this work Grasset was already developing an approach to natural ornament which would be fully realized in *La Plante*.

The abstraction and linearity which so appealed to Grasset in oriental and medieval art were fully exploited in his designs for stained glass and mosaic, executed by the master craftsman Felix Gaudin and regarded by contemporaries as amongst the artist's finest works. In the 1880s and 1890s Louis Comfort Tiffany introduced new colours and textures into the process of glass making, by which he helped to establish a major vogue for this medium. Much of Grasset's graphic work in the 1890s is therefore in a style either directly intended for, or related to, stained glass. Many of the illustrations in *La Plante* can be seen within this trend, and the richness of their colour frequently evokes glasswork.

A teacher as well as an artist, Grasset wrote and spoke at some length on his notions of the centrality of ornament to design, of its relationship to nature and the artist's observation of the natural world. His theories of the 1890s were skilfully summarized by Ferdinand Weyl in an important article on the artist published in *L'Art et la Vie* in 1894. Weyl explains: 'There are several ways of imitating nature; the artist represents the model in front of his eyes in an exact fashion which could be somehow photographic; he can also interpret it, that is to say accentuate, for instance certain colours, finish and complete certain movements that nature may only have sketched. Which is better of these two methods in decorative art? Grasset believes it is the second.' The argument here is that simply to copy nature is futile; a further interpretative stage is required. Weyl elaborates on the point: 'But where will the clarity of a decorative composition come from? It will obviously come from the predominance of a motif...' In the light of these ideas we can now turn to a closer examination of *La Plante* itself.

In 1897 the first volume of *La Plante* was published in Brussels, in a folio, with an introduction by Grasset and seventy-two full-page plates, hand-coloured by the stencil method known as *pochoir*. In the same year an English edition was published by Chapman and Hall, London, to be sold in twelve monthly instalments of six plates, each instalment being priced at eight shillings – a considerable sum and one which reflects the high production costs of the *pochoir* method. The British Library possesses copies of both editions in their original bindings; interestingly, the English edition used the bold, floral, strongly Art Nouveau cover design of the Belgian edition, but substituted the French typeface with a much more traditional English type which sits ill at ease in its decorative surround. In 1899 a second volume of *La Plante* was produced in Brussels and was issued in monthly instalments from 1900. The actual execution of the book was entrusted to Grasset's most promising senior students whose signatures appear on each plate. These include Maurice Pillard Verneuil who later produced his own book entitled *L'Animal dans la Décoration*, directly modelled on *La Plante*, and dedicated to Grasset who wrote a typically generous and enthusiastic introduction. Another student whose name features prominently in the second volume of *La Plante* is the young Swiss artist Augusto Giacometti,

*Opposite: Wisteria*

8

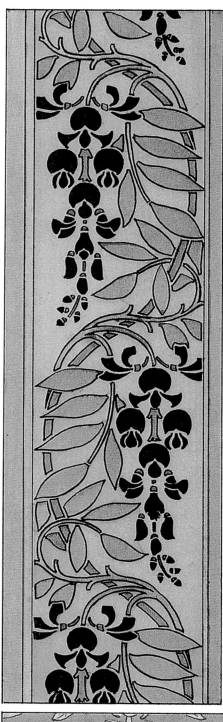

brother of the sculptor Alberto, who determined to become a pupil of Grasset's after seeing the first volume of this work.

The layout of the original book was both simple and effective. Each plant was first depicted on a full page in the manner of a botanical watercolour. Three or four subsequent plates were then devoted to developing patterns and colour combinations based on the natural structures and tones of the plant. Thus, in the original volume, the depiction of an iris was followed by a page of three designs incorporating the iris motif, one of which is included in this selection (plate 8). In this plate by M.P. Verneuil the design on the upper left strongly suggests stained glass, that on the upper right, wallpaper, and running along the bottom, a stencilled frieze. Each of these designs was juxtaposed with a verve and sensitivity to the layout of the page which is again suggestive of Grasset's debt to oriental art. The range of species thus treated was immense, covering the plant world from Arrow-head (plate 1) to Waterlily (plate 26).

The structure of *La Plante* expressed pictorially Grasset's idea on ornament as summarized by F. Weyl above. For Grasset, the starting point was nature itself, in his words: 'Nature, behold the book of ornamental art which we must consult.' Then, through a combination of the artist's imagination, his knowledge of the intended application of his design and his awareness of the art of the past, a series of ornamental variations was produced, united by a single motif. In this way a style was created, hence Grasset's definition: 'style ... is the expression of individual or collective will modifying accidental nature in works of art'.

The cogent and impassioned introduction to *La Plante* may be seen as one of Grasset's last statements in support of Art Nouveau which he was decisively to reject in a speech to the Union Centrale des Arts Décoratifs in April 1897. None of his doubts were, however, expressed in *La Plante*. According to Grasset, the artist should take as his starting point the reason and experience gained through knowledge of the art of the past, for, as he said: 'one cannot, after all, begin totally from scratch'. Nevertheless he did not advocate copying. Rather he considered it a question of a return to the fundamentals or foundation of art, that being nature itself. This was the aim to which Grasset aspired over his long career and which he set up as a goal to his students whom he engaged in what he described as 'a ceaseless struggle against mere imitation of past styles'. The almost infinite possibilities inherent in the structure of *La Plante* were stressed by its designer; he had, he said, provided almost one hundred and fifty designs ready for execution, but which the enthusiastic reader could regard merely as a starting point from which to make variations. Seen in these terms, it is not surprising that *La Plante* was to prove such a successful and influential work. Grasset concluded his introduction with a fervent plea for the primacy of colour, asserting that it was the 'visible feeling' in design. Again it was to nature that he attributed the power to drive 'ash grey, funeral grey...anaemia' from the realms of design, substituting for these tones 'a rich and regenerated life blood'.

Grasset's theories on art and ornament were most fully expressed in a book entitled *Méthode de Composition Ornementale* published in 1905. In its introduction the artist defined the creation of ornament as 'a way of expressing our joy in living...', a sentiment which was echoed by other artists and designers of the period, including William Morris who defined art as: '... the human expression of the joy of labour, done by the people for the people, is a joy for he who makes it and he who uses it ...' Morris's sentiments here are close to those expressed by Grasset when he states that his book is but a starting point for creativity.

*La Plante* was not the first nor only book of its kind; among the numerous pattern books based on floral ornament produced between 1875 and 1900 were those of A. Seder: *Die Pflanze in Kunst und Gewerbe* (1886); M. Meurer: *Planzenformen* (1895), and M.P. Verneuil (Grasset's protégé): *Etude de la Plante, son application aux industries d'art* (1900). It was undoubtedly, however, one of the finest examples, not only for the beauty, variety, and ingenuity of its illustrations but for its theoretical coherence, expressing as it does the deeply felt views of one of the great masters of French Art Nouveau design.

The group of plates reproduced in this edition have been carefully selected to give the flavour of Grasset's original volumes. They have all been drawn from the 'developed design' plates and thus form a compendium of decorative motifs and suggestions for colour schemes in a way which reflects Grasset's intentions in the creation of *La Plante*.

LAURA SUFFIELD

PLATE 1
# ARROW-HEAD

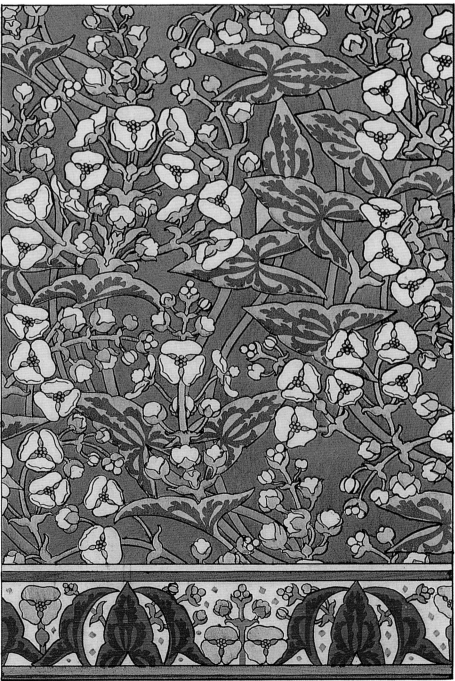

PLATE 2
# BRYONY

PLATE 3
# CHESTNUT TREE

PLATE 4
# CYCLAMEN

PLATE 5
# GERANIUM

PLATE 6
# GOURD

PLATE 7
# GOURD

C.G.-Schlum -

PLATE 8
# IRIS

PLATE 9
# FIVE-LEAVED IVY

PLATE 10
# JONQUIL

# PLATE 11
# LILAC

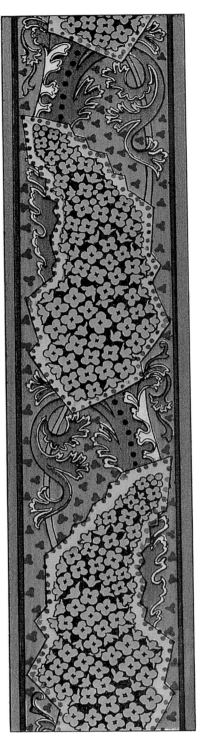

PLATE 12
# LILY OF THE VALLEY

PLATE 13
# MONKSHOOD

PLATE 14
# NASTURTIUM

## PLATE 15
# NASTURTIUM

# PLATE 16
## OAK

PLATE 17
# PERIWINKLE

PLATE 18
# POPPY

PLATE 19
# POPPY

PLATE 20
# UMBELLATED RUSH

## PLATE 21
# SNOWDROP

PLATE 22
# SNOWDROP

PLATE 23
**SORB**

PLATE 24
# SORB

PLATE 25
# SUNFLOWER

MRVerneuil.95